COMPASSION FATIGUE

WHEN POURING OUT LEAVES YOU EMPTY

DR. STUART A. MONCRIEFFE

Compassion Fatigue: When Pouring Out Leaves You Empty

ISBN: 979-8-9883287-5-9 (Paperback)

LEGAL DISCLAIMER:

The publisher and author have made every effort to ensure the information in this book is accurate. However, they make no warranties as to the completeness of the information herein and hence hereby disclaim any liability to any party for any loss, damage, or disruption caused by errors or omissions, whether such errors or omissions result from negligence, accident, or any other cause.

www.globalscribespublications.com

Table of Contents

A Note from the Author

This book was birthed out of my own journey through the academic and spiritual terrain of compassion fatigue. While completing my doctoral dissertation, I found myself intrigued by the topic, *Compassion Fatigue*. I saw clearly how the demands placed upon spiritual leaders often exceed what is humanly sustainable, especially when there are few safe spaces to rest, recover, or to be transparent.

What began as a scholarly investigation became a personal reckoning and, eventually, a prophetic assignment. I realized that far too many gifted men and women of God are suffering in silence, dying emotionally while living sacrificially. That is not God's will.

This book is my offering to the Body of Christ. It is a bridge between research and revelation, between academic language and spiritual insight. It is my prayer that as you read these pages, you will find language for your pain, strategy for your healing, and a renewed commitment to protect the vessel that God has chosen to pour through you.

You are not alone. You are not weak. You are worthy of rest.

Let us journey together toward wholeness.

With grace and strength,

-Dr. Stuart A. Moncrieffe

Introduction: For the One Who Keeps Pouring

Ministry is beautiful. It is a calling of compassion, a privilege to walk with people through the highest of joys and the deepest of sorrows. But there is a truth we don't talk about enough: you can be anointed, called, and exhausted all at the same time.

This book is for the leader who shows up, week after week, with a word on your tongue but weariness in your soul. It is for the intercessor who prays for everyone else but cries alone. It is for the shepherd who lays down their life for the sheep and wonders if anyone even notices the bruises under the robe.

You may not have had the language for it, but perhaps you've felt it; the tiredness that sleep does not fix. The irritability that sneaks in during moments of supposed joy. The disconnection you feel while preaching sermons that once ignited fire in your spirit. You love God, and you love His people but lately, ministry feels more like a burden than a blessing.

What you are feeling has a name; it is termed *compassion fatigue.*

Compassion fatigue is what happens when you pour and pour, without ever truly refilling. It is more than burnout, it is the slow erosion of joy, empathy, and spiritual strength caused by carrying the weight of other people's pain. It does not mean you're weak, unfaithful, or spiritually immature. It means you're human.

Too many pastors, leaders, and caregivers suffer silently. We keep working through the weariness, preaching while bleeding, counseling while collapsing inside, hoping no one notices that we're not okay. We believe we have to push through because "the calling is greater." But God never asked us to sacrifice our soul to serve Him.

In fact, Jesus modeled a different rhythm. He preached, He healed, He cast out demons, but He also withdrew to quiet places to rest! He honored the Sabbath. He surrounded Himself with a team. Even the Son of God did not do ministry alone or on empty.

This book is your invitation to acknowledge the issue and return to *wholeness.*

It will condemn you for being tired. It will not burden you with more "to-do" lists. Instead, it will walk with you through understanding your emotional and spiritual limits, dismantling unhealthy expectations, and rebuilding your life and ministry on a foundation of rest, boundaries, and Spirit-led care. Etched within the pages of the last chapter is also a self-check questionnaire that will help you identify how fatigued or frustrated you are.

Whether you are a senior pastor, a church leader, a counselor, or simply a person who's always "on call" for others, this book is for you. It is for every shepherd who has felt the silent weight of being everything for everyone. You can be effective and whole. You can be gifted and rested. You can lead from a place of overflow, not depletion. So breathe. You're not alone. Let us begin the journey back to strength, sanity, and spiritual vitality; not by doing more, but by learning to rest well.

1

When Pouring Out Leaves You Empty

Ministry can feel like a sacred marathon; one that never stops. The expectations to always be available, compassionate, prepared, and spiritually strong can stretch even the most committed leader beyond healthy limits. At first, you serve out of overflow. You feel joy in preaching, purpose in counseling, and fulfillment in pouring into others. But over time, without consistent replenishment, that joy can quietly fade. The energy you once had is replaced with weariness. The excitement becomes obligation. And the voice inside begins to whisper, *"I'm tired."*

This is not just tiredness that a nap can fix. It is something deeper, something called *compassion fatigue*, a slow erosion of your ability to care, connect, and minister with clarity and joy.

Compassion fatigue is emotional and spiritual depletion caused by prolonged exposure to others' pain. It often affects those who are the most loving, the most giving, the most faithful, because they care deeply, they carry deeply. And when the weight of what they carry is never lifted, when they are rarely poured into but constantly poured out, something begins to unravel.

Ministers, counselors, caregivers, and intercessors are especially vulnerable. We engage in emotionally intense moments, death beds, abuse disclosures, marriage crises, spiritual warfare; all while still needing to prepare sermons, manage church issues, and respond to the needs of our families. The very people who offer healing are often bleeding inside.

Psychologist Christina Maslach, one of the leading voices in burnout research, describes three key elements of what she calls occupational burnout: emotional exhaustion, depersonalization, and a reduced sense of personal accomplishment. In ministry terms, that means:

- You feel drained beyond your capacity to recover.
- You begin to withdraw emotionally from the people you once felt called to love.
- You wonder if your work even makes a difference anymore.

When these three factors converge, the result is not just discouragement, it is a spiritual fog. You preach and prophesy but still feel disconnected from the words coming out of your mouth. You counsel but resent the phone ringing again from anyone who needs counseling. You worship but feel numb. You give and give but no longer know how to receive.

This is not failure. This is not backsliding. This is not a lack of faith.

This is the toll of sustained emotional labor without recovery.

Even biblical giants reached this place. Elijah, after his greatest prophetic showdown, *"went a day's journey into the wilderness, and came and sat down under a broom tree. And he prayed that he might die, and said, 'It is enough! Now, Lord, take my life, for I am no better than my fathers!'"* (1 Kings 19:4, NKJV). Elijah was not lazy, he was exhausted. And the first thing God did was not rebuke him but allow him to rest.

Moses cried out in Numbers 11:14, *"I am not able to bear all these people alone, because the burden is too heavy for me."* Even Moses, the great deliverer, felt the crushing weight of leading people who were constantly in need. And God answered by appointing seventy others to help carry the load.

Paul's truth coined in his writing in 2 Corinthians 1:8 (NKJV), said, *"We were burdened beyond measure, above strength, so that we despaired even of life."* Paul, the apostle of faith and power, reached a moment where he felt broken under the pressure.

God never rebuked these men for being overwhelmed. He met them in their fatigue, provided divine assistance, and reminded them of their humanity.

To the weary soul, Jesus extends this same invitation: *"Come to Me, all you who labor and are heavy laden, and I will give you rest."* (Matthew 11:28, NKJV). Rest is not optional in ministry; it is God's response to your humanity.

"He gives power to the weak, and to those who have no might He increases strength." (Isaiah 40:29, NKJV)

"Even the youths shall faint and be weary, and the young men shall utterly fall, but those who wait on the Lord shall renew their strength." (Isaiah 40:30–31, NKJV)

The Lord sees your labor. He knows the late nights, the silent tears, the hidden burdens. And He's not asking you to keep pushing through the pain. He's calling you back to rest, reset, and be restored.

You do not have to minister from an empty place. You do not have to accept depletion as your normal. And you do not have to carry the weight of the world on shoulders that were never meant to bear it alone.

God has made a way for your recovery. But first, you must admit that you're tired; not because you're failing, but because you've been faithful. You've poured much. Now it is time to be poured into.

2

The Silent Pain of the Pulpit

There is a unique kind of pain that comes with ministry, one not easily articulated, often dismissed, and frequently hidden behind polished sermons, pressed garments, and perfected smiles. It is the kind of pain that rarely makes its way into prayer requests or pastoral meetings because it lives in the shadows. This is the silent pain of the pulpit.

Every week, leaders mount pulpits and platforms to deliver a word from God. They teach, preach, exhort, and counsel. They dedicate babies, officiate weddings, preach funerals, and visit hospitals. They carry the spiritual weight of a people, often without ever voicing the burden of their own soul. Beneath the anointing, behind the titles, beneath the training and gifting, is a human heart, one that often beats heavy with unprocessed grief, fatigue, and internal conflict.

This chapter is for the ones who have learned to function while bleeding. The ones who have felt like Elijah; bold one moment, broken the next. The ones who pour out revelation from an empty well, not because they're rebellious or faithless, but because no one notices when they are drowning quietly. The ones who dare not say "I'm tired" because too many people rely on them to be okay.

There is a cultural and theological pressure that rests heavily on those who serve the Church. In many congregations, especially in tight-knit or traditional communities, pastors are viewed as untouchable pillars of spiritual strength. They are expected to always be available, always wise, always discerning, always full. And while it is noble to strive toward integrity and excellence, it becomes dangerous when humanity is sacrificed on the altar of perfection.

Scripture never portrays leaders as superheroes. In fact, one of the great strengths of the Bible is how transparently it depicts the weaknesses of those God called to lead. David was a man after God's own heart yet wrestled deeply with anguish and sorrow. *"I am weary with my groaning; all night I make my bed swim; I drench my couch with my tears"* (Psalm 6:6, NKJV). Jeremiah, the weeping prophet, was called to proclaim judgment and hope in the face of rejection, and he cried out, *"Woe is me, my mother, that you have borne me, a man of strife and a man of contention to the whole earth!"* (Jeremiah 15:10, NKJV). Paul, though the most prolific apostle of the New Testament, confessed, *"Besides the other things, what comes upon me daily: my deep concern for all the churches"* (2 Corinthians 11:28, NKJV).

This emotional and spiritual strain is not new. What is new is how silently leaders are suffering today and that number increases at an alarming rate daily. Unlike previous generations where communal ministry and elders provided shared responsibility, today's ministers often serve in isolation. They are expected to wear multiple hats: preacher, counselor, administrator, fundraiser, event planner, mediator, and more all while maintaining a spiritual life that appears untouched by pressure.

It is in this place of invisibility that compassion fatigue begins to incubate. Leaders carry congregational trauma, unresolved conflict, church hurt, and spiritual warfare, all without having the time, space, or safety to release what they absorb. What begins as fatigue can morph into resentment. What starts as overextension becomes disconnection. And before long, the shepherd/leader no longer recognizes the sound of their own voice in the message they're preaching.

This is where Maslach's model becomes relevant again. Emotional exhaustion, depersonalization, and the loss of a sense of accomplishment are amplified in ministry because the metrics of success are often intangible. Unlike a teacher who can measure academic progress or a nurse who can track recovery, spiritual leaders deal with matters of the heart and soul. Progress is slow, victories are unseen, and fruit is sometimes buried under layers of spiritual resistance. This uncertainty, compounded with lack of support, leads to quiet despair.

Yet the Church continues to struggle with creating safe spaces for clergy to process their pain. In some traditions, acknowledging weakness is equated with a lack of faith. Seeking therapy is viewed as spiritual compromise. Admitting struggle is seen as failure. As a result, many pastors bury their pain in productivity. They work harder, preach louder, schedule more meetings, not because they are driven by vision, but because slowing down would force them to feel what they've buried.

Theological misconceptions don't help. Many believe that sacrifice means self-neglect. That suffering silently is a virtue. That to deny oneself is to deny one's emotional and physical needs. But Jesus never taught martyrdom without wisdom. Yes, He said, *"Take up your cross and follow Me"* (Matthew 16:24, NKJV), but He also modeled retreating to the mountains to pray

(Luke 5:16), sleeping in the boat during storms (Mark 4:38), and asking the disciples to watch with Him in Gethsemane (Matthew 26:38). He was both divine and deeply human. And so are we.

There must come a time when the shepherd acknowledges the internal cry: *"Lord, I am weary."* There must be room in the Church for leaders to heal, rest, confess, and be cared for, not just honored on anniversaries or during clergy appreciation month, but genuinely nurtured in the spirit.

Paul said, *"Bear one another's burdens, and so fulfill the law of Christ"*(Galatians 6:2, NKJV). That command applies to pastors too. They are not exempt from needing help. They are not excluded from the ministry of comfort and care. Leaders need leaders. Shepherds need tending too.

Sometimes, the pulpit becomes a hiding place. It becomes a place where performance replaces presence. But God is not asking us to perform. He is asking us to be whole. And wholeness begins with honesty. The silence around clergy pain must be broken. Not just for the sake of the leaders, but for the sake of the Church. Because a weary shepherd cannot nourish the sheep. A bitter and broken pastor cannot preach genuinely about healing. And a burned-out prophet cannot release a pure Word.

This is why God commands rest. The Sabbath was not just ceremonial; it was protective. It was a divine interruption to human striving. *"Remember the Sabbath day, to keep it holy. Six days you shall labor... but the seventh day is the Sabbath of the Lord your God"* (Exodus 20:8–10, NKJV). Rest is holy. Rest is obedience. And for the minister, rest is survival.

To the one quietly hurting, may you know that God sees beyond your robe, your title, and your responsibilities. He sees your heart. He sees the silent tears. And He invites you to come, not with a sermon, not with a program, not with performance, just yourself. *"He restores my soul; He leads me in the paths of righteousness for His name's sake"* (Psalm 23:3, NKJV).

You do not have to bleed in silence. You do not have to keep pretending. The pulpit is not your prison. It is a platform for healing, but healing begins with you.

3

God Never Called You to Be Superhuman

There is a quiet but powerful deception that lingers in the hearts of many leaders: the belief that to be truly faithful, we must never stop. That the more we pour, the more spiritual we are. That God is most pleased when we are most always going because it is called sacrifice. This mindset has been passed down through generations, reinforced by partial interpretations of Scripture, and glamorized in church culture. But it is not the gospel. And it is not the will of God.

God never called His servants to be superhuman. He called them to be surrendered, but not self-destructive. Somewhere along the way, many leaders began to confuse divine calling with unrelenting output and outpour. They adopt a version of ministry that glorifies overworking, neglecting rest, and equating burnout with faithfulness. They wear exhaustion as a badge of honor, proudly stating how many services they have preached, how little they have slept, or how long they went without a break; ignorantly believing suffering proves our commitment. But the cross Jesus carried was not a call to ignore human limits. It was a call to obedience, not overextension.

Theologically, much of this stems from a misapplication of Scriptures that call us to deny ourselves and follow Christ. *"Then Jesus said to His disciples, 'If anyone desires to come after Me, let him deny himself, and take up his cross, and follow Me'"* (Matthew 16:24, NKJV). But self-denial is not the same as self-neglect. Jesus never denied His humanity: He rested, He wept, He withdrew, and He asked for support. The same Savior who fed the five thousand also told His disciples, *"Come aside by yourselves to a deserted place and rest a while"* (Mark 6:31, NKJV).

Rest was not a suggestion; it was a safeguard. Many ministers, especially in high-demand church cultures, are driven by the silent pressure to be all things to all people. They take on every counseling request, lead every prayer meeting, manage every detail, and feel guilty when they cannot show up. But even Paul, who said *"I have become all things to all men, that I might by all means save some"*(1 Corinthians 9:22, NKJV), did so under the guidance of the Spirit, not under compulsion or pressure to please everyone.

When we lead out of obligation rather than obedience, we begin to drift into a works-based model of ministry that slowly drains the soul. This over-functioning is often spiritualized. Leaders will say, "The Lord will strengthen me," or "His grace is sufficient." And while both statements are true, they are often used as coping mechanisms to avoid confronting unhealthy patterns. Ask me how I know, I've heard those same Word spoken to me! God's grace empowers us to fulfill our calling but not to violate the boundaries He set for our well-being.

The apostle Paul did indeed say, *"Most gladly I will rather boast in my infirmities, that the power of Christ may rest upon me"*(2 Corinthians 12:9, NKJV). But he was not boasting about working himself into the ground. He was acknowledging that divine strength shows up when human weakness is surrendered, not when it is ignored or suppressed.

One of the greatest theological shifts that needs to happen in the Church today is this: *Faithfulness does not mean constant availability. Holiness does not require exhaustion.*

We are not God. We are His vessels. And vessels must be maintained to be effective. A cracked vessel leaks. A dirty vessel contaminates. A neglected vessel eventually shatters under pressure.

The pressure to be superhuman in ministry often stems from both internal and external sources. Internally, many leaders wrestle with perfectionism and guilt. They feel like they must earn the approval of God and man through nonstop labor. Externally, congregational expectations can create unrealistic demands where members expect instant replies, flawless preaching, and emotional availability at all times. Other external issues could also be expectation outside the perimeter of ministry; family, marketplace and/or personal. This will be discussed in depth in chapter five.

In this pressure system, many pastors fall into what Maslach's model identifies as *reduced personal accomplishment*; where leaders, despite doing much and feel like they're not doing enough. But what if enough really is enough? What if God is not measuring your effectiveness by your exhaustion, but by your obedience?

The prophet Micah asked the ancient question: *"What does the Lord require of you?"* The answer simple yet profound: *"To do justly, to love mercy, and to walk humbly with your God"* (Micah

6:8, NKJV). There is no mention of working yourself into spiritual collapse. No call to carry the church on your back. Just a daily walk with God, humble, just, merciful.

God's design for ministry was never meant to be carried in isolation. Even Moses, when overwhelmed by the burdens of the people, was instructed by God to delegate. *"Gather to Me seventy men of the elders of Israel... and they shall bear the burden of the people with you, that you may not bear it yourself alone"* (Numbers 11:16–17, NKJV). God's solution for burnout has always included shared leadership and intentional rest.

Jesus, too, modeled this. Though fully divine, He chose to operate within the limitations of human flesh. He did not rush from city to city. He was not available to everyone at every moment. He even allowed Lazarus to die before arriving because *He was led by purpose, not pressure* (John 11:6). And when He was tired, He slept, even during a storm (Mark 4:38). His rest was not irresponsibility, it was revelation. It revealed a trust in the God the Father that did not require frantic activity.

So why do we think in today's society we more available than Jesus was?

The answer lies in our theology. When we have internalized the belief that sacrifice equals suffering without boundaries, we end up glorifying pain. We spiritualize burnout. And we turn ministry into martyrdom. But Scripture calls us not to die in ministry, but to live through it. *"I have come that they may have life, and that they may have it more abundantly"* (John 10:10, NKJV).

That abundant life is for pastors, too. If ministry has robbed you of peace, if preaching has stolen your joy, if serving has silenced your worship; it is time to pause. Not because you've failed, but because *you're human.* And being human is not a flaw, it is how God designed you. *"He knows our frame; He remembers that we are dust"* (Psalm 103:14, NKJV).

What God requires of you is not perfection, but surrender. Not burnout, but balance. Not relentless productivity, but faithful presence. The time has come to release the burden of being superhuman. The Church does not need another tired preacher, another emotionally distant pastor, or another silently suffering leader. The Church needs healthy vessels, leaders who walk with God, live in rest, and minister from a place of grace.

Let this be the chapter where you decide to believe that your humanity is not in conflict with your calling. That your need for rest is not weakness. That your limits are not liabilities but invitations. Invitations to depend more deeply on the One who never slumbers nor sleeps. You were never called to carry the

Kingdom on your back. You were called to carry His yoke and *His yoke is easy, and His burden is light* (Matthew 11:30, NKJV).

4

Burned Out but Still on Fire

There's a dangerous place in ministry where the heart grows tired, but the hands keep moving. Where sermons are still preached, services are still led, prayers are still prayed, but the inner well is dry. This is the place where many leaders find themselves burned out yet still on fire, operating in the gifts of the Spirit while slowly unraveling within.

This chapter is for the leader who is fully functional but spiritually fatigued. You haven't quit. You haven't walked away. You haven't even slowed down. In fact, from the outside, you still seem ablaze, anointed, impactful, productive. But beneath the performance, something is breaking. You feel emotionally numb, disconnected from joy, and tired in ways that no amount of sleep can fix.

This is the hidden side of burnout, when ministry keeps moving but your soul is shutting down.

Studies have identified this stage as one that many clergy encounter due to chronic exposure to other people's pain, unrealistic role expectations, lack of support, and blurred boundaries. These burdens build slowly. At first, it is subtle. You still love God. You still love the people. But the spark is dimming. The joy is leaking. The fire you once carried feels more like a flicker than a flame.

And yet, you continue.

This is what makes burnout in spiritual leadership so hard to detect, because it often wears a mask of excellence. You can be preaching powerfully and dying silently. You can be performing miracles for others while neglecting your own need for healing. You can be casting out devils while your own soul is being tormented by exhaustion.

The Apostle Paul wrote with painful transparency: *"We were burdened beyond measure, above strength, so that we despaired even of life"*(2 Corinthians 1:8, NKJV). This was not Paul giving up, it was Paul being honest. There comes a point in spiritual service where the pressure feels like too much. And the real danger lies not just in the weight of the burden, but in the refusal to acknowledge it.

Many clergy suffer in silence because they feel that to admit burnout is to admit weakness or defeat. But the truth is, burnout is not a sign of spiritual failure, it is a symptom of prolonged spiritual neglect.

One of the most damaging myths in ministry is the belief that anointing is enough to sustain us. That as long as we are gifted, as long as God is using us, we must be okay. But we must understand this: the gifts of God are without repentance (Romans 11:29), He may still use you while you are unraveling. That does not mean you're healthy. That means you're functional.

And functioning while unwell is not faith, it is survival.

According to Maslach's model mentioned in chapter one, burnout includes emotional exhaustion, depersonalization, and a diminished sense of personal achievement. For ministers, emotional exhaustion may look like waking up dreading another Sunday. Depersonalization may show up as emotional detachment from your congregation, you no longer feel their pain; you're just going through the motions. And the diminished sense of accomplishment? That's when the applause no longer satisfies, the growth no longer excites you, and the affirmation feels hollow.

The fire is still burning, but it is burning you.

God never intended for ministry to consume your soul. Jesus said, *"What will it profit a man if he gains the whole world, and loses his own soul?"* (Mark 8:36, NKJV). We often apply this verse to the secular world, but what about the preacher who gains a growing church but loses their emotional health? The prophet who can discern everyone else's spiritual issues but has no time to tend to their own wounds?

Ministry without rest becomes slavery. And over time, slavery breaks the spirit.

In 1 Kings 19, we meet Elijah, fresh off calling fire from heaven. He had just confronted false prophets, turned a nation back to God, and demonstrated supernatural power. Yet, one chapter later, Elijah is running into the wilderness, depressed, disillusioned, and ready to die. *"It is enough! Now, Lord, take my life"* (1 Kings 19:4, NKJV). Elijah was still on fire, but burned out.

What did God do? He did not send another assignment. He did not rebuke him. He let him rest. He sent an angel with food. He gave him time to recover before sending him back into service.

Sometimes, the most spiritual thing you can do is take a nap and eat a meal.

Burnout also distorts your perception. It causes you to believe lies like, "I'm alone," "I'm failing," or "God is done with me." That's what Elijah believed too. He said, *"I alone am left"*(1 Kings 19:10, NKJV). But God corrected him, there were seven thousand others who hadn't bowed to Baal. Burnout creates isolation in the mind before it ever shows up in behavior.

It convinces you that your only value is in your output. That your worth is tied to your usefulness. That your call requires you to be on at all times. And that if you stop, the whole thing will fall apart.

But none of that is true.

You were not called to be a machine. You were called to be a vessel, filled, poured out, and then filled again. God never asked you to die a slow death in ministry. He came that you might have life, and life more abundantly (John 10:10).

It is possible to serve without being swallowed by service. It is possible to care deeply without being crushed by others' pain. It is possible to lead faithfully and live joyfully.

But it begins with honesty.

You must stop pretending that being "on fire" means you're whole. Some of the most anointed people in the Bible were also some of the most human. David danced before the Lord, and wept in caves. Jeremiah prophesied judgment, and asked God to kill him. Paul wrote letters of power, and confessed deep distress. Jesus healed multitudes, and then slipped away to lonely places.

Wholeness does not mean you never get tired. It means you know how to return to the One who restores your soul.

Burnout thrives in isolation. It grows in silence. But healing begins in confession. *"Come to Me, all you who labor and are heavy laden, and I will give you rest"* (Matthew 11:28, NKJV). That invitation still stands. For every pastor. Every counselor. Every leader. Every intercessor. God is not asking you to keep the fire going. He's asking you to return to the source.

You don't have to choose between your calling and your health. You can have both. But not without boundaries. Not without rest. Not without honesty.

You may be burned out, but you're not disqualified. You may feel numb, but you're not forgotten. And though you've kept the fire burning on the altar, now God wants to rekindle the fire in you. Let Him.

5

The Emotional Weight of Ministry

Ministry is not just spiritual, it is profoundly emotional. Every call, every crisis, every conversation with a grieving family or hurting soul leaves an imprint. To stand at the altar and minister to others is to constantly absorb the heartbreak, trauma, and weariness of people's lives. And while we are called to carry one another's burdens, leaders are often left holding more weight than their hearts were meant to carry alone.

The emotional weight of ministry is rarely visible. It does not announce itself. It does not bleed openly like a physical wound. It accumulates quietly. One funeral after another. One failed marriage after another. One desperate prayer request after another. You hold people together when they fall apart. You comfort others while your own grief sits in silence. You show up to offer peace while your own soul wrestles with unrest. And you do it all with a smile, because "this is what we're called to do."

But the question is: who's carrying the carrier?

The Apostle Paul said, *"We who are strong ought to bear with the failings of the weak"*(Romans 15:1, NIV). Yes, ministry requires strength. But strength without release becomes strain. And prolonged strain becomes suffering. Leaders are not just giving messages, they are absorbing sorrow, trauma, and the emotional residue of broken humanity. What starts as empathy can turn into what psychologists call secondary traumatic stress, or what is deemed has compassion fatigue.

Secondary trauma is the internal toll you pay when you listen to pain that is not your own, over and over again. It is when you counsel a woman through abuse and feel emotionally exhausted afterward. It is when you sit with a grieving father and later dream of his pain. It is when you pray for the family who just lost their child and feel the weight of that loss in your body, as if it happened to you. You are not imagining this. You are absorbing it.

Scripture calls us to weep with those who weep (Romans 12:15). But it does not ask us to drown with them. And yet, that's what often happens to those in ministry. You begin to feel everything.

Carry everything. Be everything. And in the process, you lose sight of yourself.

Jesus felt deeply. When Lazarus died, *"Jesus wept"* (John 11:35, NKJV). When He looked over Jerusalem, He cried out in anguish (Luke 19:41). But Jesus also knew when to retreat. He did not stay in the place of sorrow; He moved between the crowd and solitude. He ministered, and then withdrew. He poured out, and then reconnected with the Father. This rhythm is missing in the lives of many leaders today.

Too often, we believe that true leadership means staying accessible, never declining a request, always responding, always giving. But what's the cost? Emotional depletion. Compassion numbness. Sleepless nights. Anxious thoughts. Headaches that never go away. Ministry that once stirred your heart now weighs like a burden.

Unlike secular professionals who can compartmentalize their roles, clergy often live inside the same community they serve. That means there is no real "off-switch." You preach to people you've buried. You counsel people who have hurt you. You pray for people whose pain you carry like a secret. You hold others' storms inside your own chest, and never fully process them.

Over time, this emotional weight causes a shift. You begin to withdraw emotionally, not because you don't care, but because you've run out of room to carry anything else. You may begin to feel disconnected from your own emotions, flat in your responses, slow to engage with new people. Your mind feels foggy. Your body tightens. You start avoiding certain phone calls. You delay appointments. You dread another counseling session.

This is not laziness. This is overload.

One of the most dangerous patterns in ministry is continuing to take on new burdens while carrying unresolved pain. Trauma that is not released becomes trauma that is relived. And ministry done from an overloaded heart becomes shallow, reactive, and weary. That's not what God desires for His servants.

The Psalmist wrote, *"Cast your burden on the Lord, and He shall sustain you; He shall never permit the righteous to be moved"* (Psalm 55:22, NKJV). God never intended for you to carry burdens that He alone is equipped to bear. Yes, you are a shepherd. But you are not the Savior.

And that's the subtle deception, thinking that the more you carry, the more you reflect Christ. But Jesus did not carry every emotional wound in real-time. He carried the weight of sin once, for all. And He calls us to cast our burdens upon Him. Not hold them. Not manage them. Cast them.

"Come to Me, all you who labor and are heavy laden, and I will give you rest"(Matthew 11:28, NKJV). That invitation is not just for your members. It is for you.

Emotional weight left unchecked will eventually affect your spiritual sensitivity. What once moved you to tears may now leave you numb. What once inspired prayer may now feel like routine. What once excited you about God's people may now frustrate you. And when this begins to happen, it is not time to quit, it is time to pause. To heal. To be honest.

The Church has too many burned-out leaders still functioning, still preaching, still serving, but hollow on the inside. That is not the model Christ gave us.

In Numbers 11, Moses finally broke under the weight of leadership. He cried out, *"I am not able to bear all these people alone, because the burden is too heavy for me"*(Numbers 11:14, NKJV). God's response was not to shame Moses. It was to share the load. God appointed seventy elders to help. Because no one was meant to carry ministry alone.

You may need to do the same.

Who counsels you? Who prays for you, not just with you? Who can you tell when the emotional weight becomes too much? If the answer is no one, you are on dangerous ground.

Spiritual leadership must never come at the cost of your emotional stability. The Lord is not asking you to sacrifice your soul for your service. He is asking you to serve with wisdom. To care from a place of being cared for. To lead from a heart that is not just full of words, but full of life.

God is not glorified by leaders who collapse under unspoken pain. He is glorified when His servants walk in truth, wholeness, and peace. *"Beloved, I pray that you may prosper in all things and be in health, just as your soul prospers"* (3 John 1:2, NKJV). That includes emotional health.

You are not weak for being tired. You are not unfaithful for needing help. You are not unfit for ministry because you feel heavy.

You are simply human.

And God has made provision for that humanity. He has made space for you to be restored. He has promised to uphold you. But you must bring the weight to Him.

So take the burdens, every grief, every trauma, every broken story you've carried, and lay them down. The Cross is still strong enough to hold what your heart can no longer carry.

Ministry is demanding, but it does not exist in isolation. Behind every sermon preached, every counseling session offered, and every crisis prayer answered is a human being with a life outside of church walls. And for many clergy, the weight of ministry does not end at the pulpit, it follows them home.

One of the overlooked contributors to compassion fatigue is the collision of personal struggles with professional responsibilities. Leaders are not only pastors; they are spouses, parents, sons, daughters, and friends. They face the same family pressures and external challenges as everyone else, marriage conflicts, rebellious children, financial hardship, illness, grief, strained relationships, and yet they are often expected to carry them silently.

When the home ceases to be a place of refuge, it becomes another battlefield. A weary pastor may leave a counseling session with a grieving family only to return to arguments at home. They may spend hours tending to church needs while neglecting their own children, leaving behind unspoken guilt and regret. Financial struggles may add a layer of constant anxiety, especially in ministries where income is unstable or dependent on the generosity of others.

The overlap between ministry stress and personal stress creates a double burden:

- **Emotional Spillover:** When personal life is turbulent, leaders have fewer emotional resources to give to their congregations, making compassion fatigue set in more quickly.

- **Suppressed Struggles:** Many feel they cannot share their personal pain for fear of losing credibility or being judged unfit to lead.

- **False Expectations:** Congregations often assume pastors have perfect homes, perfect marriages, and perfect children. The gap between reality and expectation becomes a silent torment.

- **No True Place to Rest:** If both church and home feel like work, there is nowhere left to exhale, leaving leaders emotionally suffocated.

Scripture shows that even great men and women of God carried personal burdens. The Apostle Paul wrote, *"Besides everything else, I face daily the pressure of my concern for all the churches"* (2 Corinthians 11:28, NIV). Paul admitted that his spiritual assignment weighed on him daily, but it was not his only hardship, he endured physical pain, betrayals, loneliness, and personal trials. The pressures of life and ministry often collided.

Clergy need permission and support to acknowledge that personal pain affects their ability to minister effectively. Healthy church cultures recognize that pastors are whole people, not just spiritual machines, and they make space for leaders to heal both privately and publicly.

When home becomes heavy, ministry feels heavier. The healer cannot pour freely from an empty or wounded heart. Compassion fatigue is rarely caused by ministry alone, it is compounded by the unseen personal battles leaders fight when no one is watching.

6

The Pressure of Culture and Religion

Not every burden in ministry is spiritual. Some are cultural. Others are psychological. And many are reinforced by long-held traditions and unspoken expectations. For clergy across different ethnic, denominational, and religious backgrounds, the experience of compassion fatigue is not just about emotional overload, it is about how suffering is perceived, processed, and silenced by the community around them.

Culture teaches us how to feel. Religion often tells us how to suffer. And when the two intersect in ministry, they can produce a version of leadership that demands endurance but denies expression. Leaders are taught to be strong, resilient, unshakable. In some communities, asking for help is perceived as weakness.

Taking a break is viewed as laziness. Crying is seen as a lack of faith. And admitting exhaustion is interpreted as failure.

This is the hidden weight of ministry, the pressure not just to serve, but to suffer silently.

In many African, Caribbean, and Latino church cultures, spiritual leaders are elevated as sacred vessels, almost untouchable in their authority. They are viewed as prayer warriors, miracle workers, and problem solvers. There is reverence, yes, but there is also pressure. In these contexts, pastors are expected to be spiritually invincible and emotionally invisible. They are not allowed to have bad days, mental health challenges, or moments of weakness. They are expected to push through everything. Smile through the pain. Preach through the storm. And carry everyone's burdens while never naming their own.

This expectation is reinforced by a communal mindset, where the needs of the group are placed above the needs of the individual. While this has benefits, it often results in leaders neglecting their personal well-being for the sake of the collective. When the pastor suffers, the congregation often does not know. And if they do know, they expect him or her to "pray through it" rather than seek professional help or rest.

In Western, individualistic cultures, the experience of compassion fatigue may be more openly discussed, but the isolation is just as real. Leaders are often expected to self-manage without community support. The value of independence often means that struggling leaders feel ashamed to reach out or fear being seen as spiritually disqualified. The culture may say, "It is okay to talk about it," but the systems rarely make room for restoration.

In both environments, communal or individualistic, the outcome is the same: leaders who are emotionally exhausted and spiritually discouraged, with no safe place to fall apart.

Scripture shows us something different. Even Moses, revered by Israel, admitted when the burden was too heavy. *"I am not able to bear all these people alone, because the burden is too heavy for me"* (Numbers 11:14, NKJV). He was honest. Transparent. Human. And God's answer was not rebuke, it was support. *"I will take of the Spirit that is upon you and will put the same upon them; and they shall bear the burden of the people with you"* (v. 17). God responded with shared leadership, not shame.

But in many modern church settings, the idea of shared leadership is resisted. The leader is expected to be everything, preacher, counselor, administrator, intercessor, encourager, decision-maker, and even personal therapist to the congregation. The emotional labor is immense, but the permission to rest is absent.

This is especially true for women in ministry, who often face a double burden. Not only are they expected to serve with excellence, but they are also pressured to maintain emotional composure, nurture others constantly, and defy stereotypes that question their authority. The cultural and gender dynamics amplify the expectation that they must "do more to prove they belong." The result? Burnout masked by performance. Emotional fatigue hidden behind excellence.

Religion, when misapplied, can also reinforce unhealthy beliefs about pain and rest. Many leaders have been taught that enduring suffering without complaint is a spiritual virtue. That if they are truly faithful, they will carry the cross of ministry without flinching. But Jesus never asked His disciples to suffer in silence. He modeled rest. He practiced solitude. He asked for support. *"My soul is exceedingly sorrowful, even to death. Stay here and watch with Me"* (Matthew 26:38, NKJV). Even the Son of God did not suffer alone.

Too often, we spiritualize suffering in a way that glorifies overwork and self-neglect. Leaders quote verses like, *"I can do all things through Christ who strengthens me"* (Philippians 4:13, NKJV) but use them to justify taking on more than God ever intended. The truth is, yes, God strengthens us. But He also commands rest, honors boundaries, and invites healing.

When leaders internalize the idea that they must "die daily" in ministry, they often ignore the balance between sacrificial service and personal care. The apostle Paul did say, *"I die daily"* (1 Corinthians 15:31), but he was speaking of surrendering his flesh to the will of God, not of running himself into physical and emotional collapse. Paul also wrote, *"Do you not know that your bodies are temples of the Holy Spirit? Therefore, honor God with your bodies"* (1 Corinthians 6:19–20, NIV). Honoring your body includes resting it. Feeding it. Protecting it from constant strain.

My research also pointed out that theological views on suffering differ across religious traditions, and this shapes how clergy handle fatigue. In some beliefs, suffering is seen as redemptive, something to be embraced, not avoided. And while there is spiritual truth in endurance, there is also divine wisdom in knowing when to pause. Suffering is part of ministry, but suffering without care is unsustainable.

What we need is a theology of balance, a biblical framework that honors both sacrifice and stewardship. A theology that allows leaders to say, "I need help," without shame. A theology that recognizes vulnerability as strength. A theology that creates space in our churches for pastors to rest, counselors to receive counsel, and intercessors to be held.

One of the most liberating truths for any leader to accept is this: you are not your culture's expectations. You are not your congregation's demands. You are God's child first. His servant second.

God never asked you to prove your worth through pain. He proved your worth through the Cross. You don't have to bleed out in silence to validate your calling. You are already chosen. Already loved. Already accepted.

Let this be the generation of leaders who choose wholeness over image. Who reject the lie that says suffering alone is noble. Who build churches that don't just celebrate ministry gifts but protect the vessels who carry them.

Let this be the generation that teaches its leaders: *"It is okay to not be okay."*

Because it is.

"He heals the brokenhearted and binds up their wounds"(Psalm 147:3, NKJV). That promise is not just for your congregation. It is for you.

Compassion fatigue does not exist in a vacuum. It is shaped by the cultures we come from and the doctrines we're taught. For clergy, the emotional and spiritual strain of ministry is often intensified, not only by what they do, but by what their culture expects them to be. Whether it is the call to strength, silence, or service, leaders carry more than just spiritual responsibility. They carry the unspoken weight of their people's expectations.

In every context, culture teaches what is acceptable to feel and express. Religion, meanwhile, interprets what is acceptable to endure. When both systems are shaped by survival and sacrifice, as they often are, clergy are left with very little room to be human.

Let us walk through how cultural and religious backgrounds shape how leaders experience exhaustion, manage pain, and navigate burnout.

In African and African-American Churches: The Honor of Endurance

In African and African-American religious traditions, the pastor is often far more than a preacher. He or she is a community leader, intercessor, therapist, advocate, and activist. The Black church, born in the crucible of colonialism and slavery, became a sanctuary of survival and a beacon of hope. Naturally, the pastor became its spiritual and cultural backbone. And because of that, strength was never optional, it was essential.

In many African contexts, spirituality is deeply communal. Leaders are expected to pray for the sick, feed the hungry, and confront spiritual forces. They are often on call day and night. To say "no" is nearly unthinkable, and to take rest may be perceived as negligence.

In African-American churches, that same dynamic evolved in a different soil: shaped by systemic racism, generational trauma, and social marginalization. The pastor is often one of the few stable figures in the community. As a result, there's pressure to remain strong at all times. Emotional vulnerability is sometimes confused with weakness. Leaders are expected to "press through," often without emotional support or therapeutic care.

And so, many suffer in silence. They keep going until they break down. The congregation loves them, but often unknowingly contributes to their burnout, because when a shepherd never bleats, the sheep assume all is well.

In Caribbean Churches: The Expectation of Constant Spiritual Performance

In Caribbean Pentecostal and Charismatic churches, pastors are revered as fiery vessels, spiritual warriors who are always filled, always present, and always victorious. The culture values spiritual fervor and visible expressions of power. Worship is passionate. Preaching is high-intensity. Prayer is warfare. Leaders are expected to embody this spiritual charge, often without pause.

But this intensity has a cost. Caribbean pastors often serve multiple roles in small or mid-sized churches without administrative teams, counseling support, or sabbatical structures. They preach, visit, officiate, counsel, and carry family burdens, all under the weight of a theological framework that spiritualizes fatigue. Tiredness is often interpreted as spiritual attack. Burnout is seen as a demonic problem rather than a human one. Leaders learn to pray harder, fast longer, and keep going.

This creates a culture where the appearance of spiritual strength overrides emotional honesty. Admitting burnout might risk being seen as "not strong enough for the anointing." So pastors internalize their suffering, and no one notices, until something breaks.

But even Jesus, the most anointed of all, withdrew. He walked away from crowds (Luke 5:16), slept through storms (Mark 4:38), and declined certain ministry demands to preserve His focus. His humanity was not a weakness. It was wisdom. Caribbean pastors must be taught that rest is not rebellion, and that silence about one's suffering does not serve the Church; it slowly drains it.

In Latino Churches: The Burden of Spiritual Fatherhood

In many Latino churches, ministry is deeply familial. The pastor is not just a preacher, he is *Padre*, spiritual father, caregiver, and emotional anchor. Congregations often see the clergy as part of the extended family, which creates beautiful, intimate church life, but also brings an enormous emotional burden.

In immigrant churches, especially, the pastor helps with everything: immigration paperwork, translation, housing crises, domestic violence issues, and more. The boundary between personal life and pastoral duty is almost non-existent. There's an expectation to always be available, to answer every call, show up at every home, attend every emergency.

This is compounded by a cultural reverence for *suffering as sanctification*. Pain is often spiritualized, and the Cross is interpreted as a lifelong calling to sacrifice, emotionally, physically, and financially. Pastors may feel guilty for needing rest. They may struggle to say "I need help," fearing that it means they are not faithful enough.

What gets lost in this sacrificial culture is the truth that God does not require pastors to die slowly to prove their loyalty. Yes, Christ suffered. Yes, we carry crosses. But leadership is not meant to destroy the vessel. Paul said, *"We have this treasure in jars of clay"* (2 Corinthians 4:7). Even clay cracks when not cared for.

The Latino church must relearn that self-care is not selfish, it is sacred stewardship of a body and soul entrusted by God.

In Western Churches: The Pressure to Perform

In North American and European church cultures, clergy often face pressure not from community need but from performance metrics. Success is measured in data: attendance, budgets, engagement. Pastors are not just spiritual leaders, they're expected to be CEOs, visionaries, entrepreneurs, digital content creators.

In this landscape, burnout comes wrapped in productivity. You can be emotionally depleted but still considered "effective" as long as the numbers are rising. Western culture prizes individualism, which means many pastors are isolated. They lead in competitive environments where vulnerability may cost them respect or opportunity.

Theological language does not always help. Scriptures like *"I can do all things through Christ"* are quoted to justify overextension.

Many leaders ignore their limits until they collapse, privately or publicly.

But God never measured faithfulness by busyness. He measured it by obedience. *"Unless the Lord builds the house, those who build it labor in vain"* (Psalm 127:1). Western churches must begin creating systems where ministry is not sustained by hustle, but by health.

In East Asian Churches: The Quiet Weight of Honor

In East Asian cultures, particularly among Chinese, Korean, and Japanese churches, ministry is often guided by values of discipline, hierarchy, and honor. The pastor is highly respected, and with that honor comes a silent expectation: control your emotions. Do not show weakness. Maintain composure.

The concept of *"saving face"* influences how leaders manage stress. Expressing emotional exhaustion may be seen as shameful or ungrateful. Many pastors internalize their struggles, believing that endurance without complaint is a sign of maturity.

In such cultures, suffering is endured stoically, but at a deep cost. Burnout manifests not through outbursts but through physical ailments, withdrawal, and quiet despair. Depression may go undiagnosed. Marriages quietly suffer. Pastors suffer inwardly while smiling publicly.

The gospel offers a different picture. Christ, in Gethsemane, did not save face, He bled it. He wept openly. He asked for help. East Asian pastors must be given permission to do the same. Jesus modeled a humanity that did not threaten His holiness, and neither will yours.

In Indigenous Churches: The Burden of Restoration

For Indigenous pastors, ministry is often intertwined with cultural and communal healing. Many serve people who carry deep generational trauma, loss of land, language, identity, and ancestral connection. The church is not just a place of worship, but a space to reclaim dignity and rebuild community.

The Indigenous pastor is not only a spiritual leader but also a cultural preserver. They carry stories, mediate conflict, bury elders, and often bridge the gap between ancient tradition and Christian practice. This emotional and cultural labor is immense.

But most Indigenous pastors work in under-resourced contexts. They serve in remote areas, with little to no access to counseling or pastoral care. Their suffering is quiet, but historic. Compassion fatigue here is layered with grief, not just personal, but generational.

And yet, even here, God speaks: *"He heals the brokenhearted and binds up their wounds"* (Psalm 147:3). Indigenous leaders must be supported, not only with spiritual tools, but with cultural understanding and systems of rest that honor their heritage.

Let the Silence End

What unites all these contexts is one painful truth: clergy are suffering silently under the weight of cultural and religious pressure. They are praised for endurance but punished for pausing. They are expected to give endlessly and grieve invisibly.

But Christ's yoke is easy. His burden is light.

Let this be the generation that redefines strength, not as silence, but as honesty. Not as perfection, but as presence. Not as never breaking down, but as knowing when to ask for help.

Culture may demand your silence, but Christ invites your truth. *"Come to Me, all you who labor and are heavy laden, and I will give you rest"* (Matthew 11:28). Not just for your congregation. For you.

7

Boundaries Are Biblical

In ministry, boundaries are not commonly taught, they are learned, usually the hard way. Many pastors and leaders enter ministry with the desire to serve, not realizing that the very call to serve can become a doorway to exhaustion if not guarded with wisdom. There is a difference between laying your life down for the sheep and being trampled by them. One is Christlike. The other is unhealthy.

Somewhere in the minds of many clergy, a dangerous idea takes root: that true faithfulness means never saying no. That real anointing means being endlessly available. That self-denial means self-erasure. But the truth is: God honors limits. God created boundaries. God expects you to rest.

We are vessels, not saviors. But when leaders try to function without boundaries, they end up playing God, consciously or not. And the consequences are emotional depletion, compassion fatigue, and spiritual dullness.

In my study I also highlighted the role that blurred personal-professional boundaries play in clergy burnout. When leaders are accessible 24/7, emotionally entangled in every crisis, unable to say no, and constantly adjusting their lives to meet unrealistic demands, they begin to fragment internally. Their private world shrinks. Their identity becomes wrapped in what they do. And slowly, joy begins to evaporate.

But Scripture does not call us to burnout. It calls us to obedience and order.

Even in creation, God established boundaries. He separated light from darkness, land from sea, and time for work from time for rest. He could have created everything in one breath, but He took six days. Then He rested. *"On the seventh day God ended His work... and He rested... Then God blessed the seventh day and sanctified it"*(Genesis 2:2–3, NKJV). God modeled limits before man even existed.

If the Creator of the universe honors boundaries, so should His servants.

Jesus Set Boundaries

Jesus, the very embodiment of divine compassion, did not meet every need. That truth alone should set leaders free. He healed many, but not all. He said "no" to crowds. He walked away from opportunities. He chose solitude over demand.

In Mark 1:35–38, Jesus withdrew early in the morning to pray. When the disciples found Him and said, *"Everyone is looking for You,"* Jesus replied, *"Let us go somewhere else... so I can preach there also. That is why I have come."* He did not return to the people waiting. He did not explain. He moved on, because He understood His assignment, and He did not let pressure from others redefine His mission.

Jesus often went to solitary places (Luke 5:16). He slept in the boat during a storm (Mark 4:38). He pulled away from crowds (Matthew 14:13). These were not acts of selfishness. They were acts of obedience. He knew that intimacy with the Father was more important than nonstop ministry.

How many leaders today have lost that rhythm? They serve, preach, counsel, and plan, but never withdraw. They lead meetings but not moments of stillness. They care for everyone but themselves. This is not what Jesus modeled.

Boundaries Are Not Rejection, They Are Protection

One of the deepest fears many clergy have is being perceived as uncaring. Saying no feels cruel. Rescheduling feels like neglect. Delegating feels like losing control. But the truth is, boundaries are not rejection, they are protection.

When Moses tried to carry the burden of leadership alone, his father-in-law Jethro intervened. *"What you are doing is not good,"* Jethro said. *"You and these people... will only wear yourselves out"* (Exodus 18:17–18, NIV). He instructed Moses to delegate responsibility and only handle the cases that truly needed his attention. Moses listened, and it preserved both his energy and the people's well-being.

If you don't establish boundaries, you will burn out. And eventually, the very people you're trying to serve will feel the consequences of your exhaustion.

Boundaries protect:

- Your mental health
- Your family
- Your prayer life
- Your ability to hear God clearly
- Your joy in ministry

They are not unspiritual. They are not unloving. They are biblical.

Why Leaders Resist Boundaries

If boundaries are so vital, why do so many pastors struggle to maintain them? Because of deeply embedded fears:

- Fear of disappointing people
- Fear of being replaced
- Fear of appearing weak or lazy
- Fear of losing control
- Fear that God is only pleased when they are constantly producing

These fears often stem from internalized performance-based theology, the belief that God is most pleased when we are busiest. But Scripture says, *"Be still, and know that I am God"* (Psalm 46:10). Stillness, not busyness, is what deepens our awareness of Him.

Leaders also struggle because boundary-setting requires confrontation, not always with others, but often with self. It requires acknowledging limitations. It requires redefining your identity, not by what you do, but by who you are in Christ.

Healthy Boundaries Are a Form of Holiness

Holiness is not just moral purity. It is also being set apart. When you establish boundaries, you are not being selfish, you are preserving your sacred space. You are honoring the God who created your body, your emotions, your mind.

Paul wrote, *"Do you not know that your bodies are temples of the Holy Spirit…? Therefore, honor God with your bodies"* (1 Corinthians 6:19–20, NIV). That includes knowing when your body is tired. That includes saying no to an event so you can go for a walk, pray without a clock, or simply sleep.

Jesus honored His vessel so that it could remain a vessel. He protected His energy so He could pour with power. So must we.

What Boundaries Might Look Like

Every ministry is different. Every leader has different needs. But here are some boundaries that reflect biblical wisdom:

- **A Sabbath day** where no ministry is done, only rest.
- **Office hours** that define when you are available for meetings and calls.
- **Clear expectations** about what you can and cannot take on personally.

- **Scheduled times for prayer and solitude** that are non-negotiable.
- **Family time** that is protected from ministry demands.
- **Delegation** of tasks that others can do so you can focus on what only you are called to do.

Even the apostle Paul shared responsibility. He appointed elders, raised up Timothy, and constantly wrote about the importance of the body working together. Leaders who do not delegate are not more spiritual, they are more at risk.

A Ministry that Lasts

Ministry is not a sprint. It is a marathon. And like any marathon, pace is everything. If you run too hard, too fast, with no breaks, you will collapse before the finish line.

The Church does not need another exhausted prophet. It needs whole ones. Leaders who know when to engage, when to retreat, when to give, and when to receive.

The gospel is not advanced through burnout. It is advanced through Spirit-filled obedience, rooted in rhythms of rest.

Let this be the chapter where you give yourself permission. Permission to pause. Permission to be unavailable sometimes. Permission to protect your vessel. God is not measuring your worth by how many meetings you attend or how many sermons you preach. He is looking for your heart, your whole, healthy heart.

"Above all else, guard your heart, for everything you do flows from it"(Proverbs 4:23, NIV).

That begins with boundaries. And boundaries begin with believing you are worth protecting.

8

A Theology of Rest

For many leaders, rest feels like a reward, something earned after the work is done, if there's time left. But biblically, rest is not a reward. It is a requirement. It is built into the rhythm of creation, the law of the covenant, the life of Christ, and the health of every human soul.

Ministry can be relentless. There is always one more call, one more sermon, one more need, one more emergency. The pressure to be available, responsive, and present never fully subsides. For clergy, rest is often postponed until crisis forces it. But by then, the damage is done. Burnout has already taken root. The joy of ministry becomes a memory, and the leader becomes a shell, pouring out from a dry well, surviving on momentum, not meaning.

My research pointed to this clearly that many clergy suffer compassion fatigue not just from what they carry, but from never stopping long enough to unload. The issue is not only the weight of the work, but the refusal to pause. And that refusal is often framed as righteousness, "I will rest when the work is done," "God will strengthen me," "The enemy does not rest, so I cannot either."

But the enemy is not our example. God is.

Rest as a Spiritual Mandate

The very first time Scripture introduces the concept of rest, it is not for man, it is God Himself who rests. *"On the seventh day God ended His work which He had done, and He rested… Then God blessed the seventh day and sanctified it"* (Genesis 2:2–3, NKJV). The God who never grows weary chose to cease, not because He needed rest, but because rest is sacred. He wove it into the order of life before sin ever entered the world.

In the Decalogue, the Ten Commandments, the fourth command to "remember the Sabbath" (Exodus 20:8) comes before instructions about murder, adultery, and theft. Sabbath was not just about spiritual devotion. It was about rhythm, trust, and resistance. It was God's way of saying, "You are not machines. You are My people. And you don't belong to Pharaoh anymore."

When God delivered Israel from slavery, He did not just free their bodies. He broke their dependence on nonstop productivity. Pharaoh never gave them a day off. But God did. In fact, He commanded it. Rest was how they would remember they were no longer slaves.

And yet today, many leaders live like Pharaoh still signs their checks. Rest is ignored. Pausing is avoided. Sabbath is seen as optional. But in doing so, we miss a foundational truth: rest is not just about recovery. Rest is about remembering who we are, and who we are not.

We are not God. We are not omnipresent, omniscient, or unlimited. When leaders reject rest, they subconsciously embrace the lie that their value is tied to their productivity. That they must be available for everyone. That they alone are holding things together.

But Scripture declares otherwise. *"It is vain for you to rise up early, to sit up late, to eat the bread of sorrows; for so He gives His beloved sleep"*(Psalm 127:2, NKJV). God is not honored by your exhaustion. He is honored by your obedience. He gives rest, not as a sign of weakness, but as a mark of relationship.

The Rhythm of Christ

No one modeled sacred rhythm like Jesus. He ministered with intensity, but not with frenzy. He responded to needs, but was not ruled by them. And when it was time to withdraw, He did so without apology.

"But Jesus often withdrew to lonely places and prayed" (Luke 5:16, NIV). He separated Himself from the crowd after feeding the five thousand. He slipped away from people to spend time with the Father. Even when there were more people to heal, more sermons to preach, more disciples to train, He made time to rest.

Jesus slept in a storm (Mark 4:38). He walked away from expectations (Mark 1:35–38). He declined premature promotion when the crowd wanted to make Him king (John 6:15). In every case, He modeled restraint. He chose solitude over spectacle. Intimacy with the Father over approval from people.

If Jesus needed to rest, what makes us believe we don't?

Somewhere along the way, rest became a guilty pleasure instead of a holy practice. It became something leaders sneak in when no one's looking, or worse, a spiritual compromise. But rest is not the opposite of faithfulness, it is part of it.

When leaders ignore rest, the soul begins to harden. Compassion grows dull. Joy becomes mechanical. Worship feels obligatory. We may still preach, but without power. We may still pray, but without presence. That is the slow erosion of vitality that leads to burnout.

The tragedy is not that leaders grow tired. The tragedy is that they believe tiredness is what makes them effective. But the truth is, ministry done out of weariness often becomes survival, not service.

Sabbath, true Sabbath, is an act of war against the lie that says we are only valuable when we are producing. It is a declaration of trust that says, "God is still working even when I'm not."

Resistance, Rhythm, and Restoration

Clergy must reclaim a theology of rest, not just a lifestyle adjustment, but a deeply spiritual framework that aligns with God's original design.

This theology acknowledges three key truths:

1. **Rest is Resistance**
   In a culture that idolizes busyness, rest is a spiritual rebellion. It says, "I'm not driven by results; I'm led by relationship." When pastors unplug, step away, or

simply say, "Not today," they are declaring that God, not the grind, is their source.

2. **Rest is Rhythm**

   Sabbath was weekly for a reason. Rest is not occasional recovery, it is a lifestyle of returning to God. Whether it is a full day, a consistent morning of solitude, or a designated time of silence and renewal, leaders must build regular rhythms that restore the soul.

3. **Rest is Restoration**

   Jesus said, *"Come to Me, all you who labor and are heavy laden, and I will give you rest"* (Matthew 11:28, NKJV). That is not a metaphor. It is a promise. Rest is not passive. It is restorative. It is where God heals what ministry has drained. It is where identity is re-centered, purpose is rekindled, and joy is recovered.

Many pastors wait for vacation to rest. Others wait for breakdown. But leaders called by God should not need crisis to justify stillness. Sabbath is not earned. It is given. It is where you remember that you are not the provider, protector, or sustainer, God is. The ministry will never stop. There will always be more to do. But the voice of the Lord still echoes through the centuries: *"Be still and know that I am God"* (Psalm 46:10, NKJV). That knowing does not come in the chaos. It comes in the quiet.

You don't need to crash to qualify for rest. You don't need to justify stillness with exhaustion. Rest is your right as a child of God, your responsibility as a leader, and your resistance against a system that wants to consume you. Let the rhythm of rest return to your life. Let it cleanse you, reorder you, and remind you that God's strength is made perfect not in your constant movement, but in your willingness to stop.

9

Reclaiming Your Joy in Ministry

Ministry begins with joy. It starts with a sense of divine calling, a burning desire to serve, and the thrill of knowing that your life is being used by God to impact others. Most leaders can remember that moment, when the call became clear, when the first sermon stirred something deep, when the altar was full and the Spirit was moving. Ministry in its purest form is beautiful. But for too many, that beauty fades under the weight of burdens never meant to be carried alone.

This chapter is for those who still love God but have stopped enjoying the work. Those who haven't quit, but are going through the motions. Those who stand behind the pulpit but feel a thousand miles from their purpose. The flame is still lit, but it flickers. The joy that once carried them through long nights and hard seasons feels distant, even foreign.

Joy in ministry is not a bonus. It is not a luxury. It is a sign of spiritual health. And when joy is absent, it is a signal, something needs to be reclaimed.

Long-term compassion fatigue, boundary erosion, and over-identification with pastoral duties all contribute to emotional depletion and spiritual disconnection. Joy becomes collateral damage in a war against burnout. And in many cases, leaders feel guilty for admitting it.

But the Bible does not ask leaders to serve without joy. In fact, Scripture warns against joyless ministry. Paul instructed the Roman church to serve the Lord with gladness (Romans 12:11), and Peter told elders to shepherd "not under compulsion, but willingly… not for shameful gain, but eagerly" (1 Peter 5:2). God is not glorified by ministers who merely survive. He is glorified by those who flourish in their calling, those who lead from love, not obligation.

Rediscovering the Spark

The first step in reclaiming joy is remembering what it felt like to have it. When did ministry feel full of life? What made it fulfilling? Was it the people? The worship? The sense of purpose?

Often, joy does not disappear all at once. It fades quietly, the way daylight slips into dusk. A few extra responsibilities here. A few more crises there. A pile of expectations, unresolved grief, unspoken disappointment. And slowly, the thing that once made your heart burn now just makes your schedule full.

Joy, when lost, must be pursued, not passively hoped for, but intentionally recovered.

For some, this means making space for the parts of ministry that bring life. Not everything you do is draining. There are likely pieces of your work that still spark something in you. Identify them. Make room for them again. Perhaps it is teaching one-on-one, mentoring younger leaders, or spending time in quiet prayer. Too often, the demands of leadership push out the parts of ministry that first called us.

Jesus told the church in Ephesus, *"You have forsaken your first love. Remember therefore from where you have fallen; repent and do the works you did at first"* (Revelation 2:4–5, ESV). That's not just a word to congregations, it is a word to clergy. Sometimes, the way forward begins with going back. Not to repeat the past, but to re-engage what first stirred your soul.

Letting Go of What Joy Cannot Survive

Joy is delicate. It does not thrive in environments of constant pressure, comparison, or chaos. For joy to return, there are things that may need to be released, some of them good, some of them necessary, but none of them sustainable if they're suffocating your spirit. Clergy who continued carrying roles and responsibilities long after they had become joyless, did so as an obligation. Out of duty, they kept attending every function, managing every detail, solving every conflict. But in doing so, they exchanged joy for survival.

Sometimes reclaiming joy means confronting the fear that says, "If I stop doing this, everything will fall apart." That fear is not from God. It is rooted in control, pride, or unhealthy pressure. Ministry must be shared, delegated, and balanced if joy is to remain. Moses had to learn this lesson. When he tried to handle the people alone, his father-in-law warned him: *"You will surely wear yourself out... this thing is too heavy for you; you are not able to do it alone"* (Exodus 18:18, ESV).

Joy cannot survive in ministry that is overcrowded, unsustainable, and dependent on one person doing everything. Leadership without limits is not spiritual maturity, it is emotional erosion. This may also mean grieving what ministry has cost you. Many clergy continue to lead with unprocessed pain: betrayal, disappointment, unfulfilled expectations, strained family dynamics, or congregational hurt. These wounds become barriers to joy. They fester beneath the surface, even while you preach healing for others. But there is no joy without honesty. And sometimes, joy requires lament.

David said, *"Restore to me the joy of your salvation"* (Psalm 51:12, ESV). That prayer came from a place of repentance, not only for sin, but for drifting from the closeness he once shared with God. Joy is not simply about energy, it is about intimacy. If ministry has become routine, if the presence of God feels distant, the first thing to do is not to change assignments, but to return to the altar.

The altar is where joy begins again.

Joy and the Presence of God

Joy is not manufactured, it is received. It is a gift from God's presence. *"In Your presence there is fullness of joy"*(Psalm 16:11, ESV). That verse is not theoretical. It is practical. It means that joy is not primarily found in outcomes or accolades. It is found in nearness to God.

Many leaders lose their joy not because ministry is hard, but because their intimacy with God has been buried under responsibilities. The devotional life becomes task-oriented. Prayer becomes a chore. Scripture becomes sermon prep. But joy is relational. And relationships require time, attention, and vulnerability.

Sometimes the only way to reclaim joy is to stop everything, step back from the noise, the pace, the people, and just sit with God again. No agenda. No deadlines. Just presence. In that stillness, the soul breathes again. And in that space, the joy begins to return, not always explosively, but steadily. A quiet peace. A renewed sense of purpose. A fresh gratitude for the call. That's the restoration God offers. Not just enough to function, but enough to overflow.

Leading from Joy, Not Just for It

Joy is not just personal, it is pastoral. When leaders rediscover their joy, it spreads. Congregations feel it. Teams sense it. Ministry becomes lighter. Messages carry more weight. Worship deepens. Even conflict is handled with more grace.

Paul said, *"For the kingdom of God is not a matter of eating and drinking but of righteousness and peace and joy in the Holy Spirit"* (Romans 14:17, ESV). Ministry without joy is incomplete. It may be structured, biblical, and effective, but it will feel hollow. Joy is what makes the message believable. Joy is what makes the leader credible. When joy returns, the calling becomes a gift again, not just a responsibility. Ministry becomes a place of fulfillment, not just demand. And the leader becomes not just a servant, but a worshiper.

You were never meant to lead empty. You were never meant to survive your calling. You were meant to enjoy it, to taste the goodness of God not only in the fruit of your labor, but in the intimacy of His presence. If the joy is gone, it can return. If the flame has dimmed, it can be rekindled. God is not finished with you. But He may be inviting you to rediscover the joy that once made you say "yes" to this calling. Let Him restore it.

10

When the Healer Needs Healing

It is one thing to minister to the broken. It is another to do so while broken yourself.

This chapter is for the pastors who preach healing but haven't found space for their own. For the counselors who help others process trauma while burying their own. For the intercessors who carry the burdens of many but don't know who carries theirs.

There is a quiet crisis among spiritual leaders, many are wounded, but still working. They offer care without receiving it. They pour while empty. And while the external ministry continues, the internal life suffers. Beneath the polished sermons and the predictable strength is a reality few will admit: the healer needs healing too.

Ministry often attracts those with a deep sense of compassion. But over time, that same compassion becomes a doorway to overextension. And when leaders have no space to recover, pain accumulates, unspoken, unacknowledged, and unresolved. Studies have shown that many clergy suffer from untreated emotional wounds, partly because they believe they are not allowed to struggle, and partly because they don't know where to turn.

The problem is not the presence of pain. It is the pressure to pretend it does not exist.

In churches where strength is prized and suffering is spiritualized, there is rarely room for leaders to say, "I'm not okay." There is an unspoken belief that to ask for help is to lose credibility. That needing therapy means you lack faith. That counseling is for the congregation, but never for the clergy.

And so, the healer remains silent. Keeps serving. Keeps showing up. Keeps dying quietly.

The Isolation of the Anointed

One of the most misunderstood dynamics in ministry is the isolation that can come with leadership. The more influence a leader has, the fewer people they can be honest with. Friendships become complicated. Relationships shift. Conversations are filtered through roles and expectations.

Even Jesus experienced this. Though surrounded by multitudes, He often pulled away to be alone. Even among the disciples, there were only three He brought into His most vulnerable moments. And even they fell asleep when He needed them most.

In the Garden of Gethsemane, Jesus confided, *"My soul is overwhelmed with sorrow to the point of death. Stay here and keep watch with Me"* (Matthew 26:38, NIV). These are not the words of a stoic Savior. These are the words of a man who carried divine purpose and deep pain at the same time.

If Jesus could say that, if He could admit sorrow, seek companionship, and ask for prayer, why do today's leaders feel they must suffer in silence?

The answer lies in fear. Fear of losing people's respect. Fear of seeming unqualified. Fear of being misunderstood or misquoted. Fear of becoming the subject of gossip rather than the recipient of grace.

But healing begins with honesty. And honesty requires safe places, places where the leader can lay down the role and just be human again.

Every healer needs a healing space. A place where they are not expected to lead, perform, fix, or explain. A place to unravel, grieve, process, and be restored.

The tragedy is that many ministers don't have that. They are the strong one for everyone else. But no one is strong for them.

Biblical Healing for Broken Leaders

The Bible is filled with stories of people who were deeply used by God while also deeply in need of healing.

Elijah called down fire from heaven, then immediately collapsed into despair. He prayed, *"I have had enough, Lord... take my life"* (1 Kings 19:4, NIV). God did not chastise him. He fed him. Let him rest. Then gently redirected him. His healing began not with another assignment, but with rest and nourishment.

David, the warrior-king, also cried out for healing. *"Heal me, Lord, for my bones are in agony. My soul is in deep anguish. How long, Lord, how long?"* (Psalm 6:2–3, NIV). David knew how to worship, how to lead, how to fight, but he also knew how to weep. And God never turned him away for it.

The Apostle Paul experienced intense emotional pressure. *"We were under great pressure, far beyond our ability to endure, so that we despaired of life itself"* (2 Corinthians 1:8, NIV). Paul did not hide his struggle. He used it to magnify God's comfort.

Throughout Scripture, God never disqualified someone for being wounded. But He did require that wounds be acknowledged. Because God cannot heal what we pretend is not broken.

The healer's healing begins with one decision: to stop hiding pain behind productivity.

There is no shame in needing therapy. There is no shame in receiving pastoral counseling. There is no shame in admitting you are not well. What is shameful is the system that made you believe you had to deny your humanity in order to be holy.

Making Space for Recovery

The path to healing for clergy must be deliberate. It will not happen through wishful thinking or sheer willpower. It requires space, support, and surrender.

1. Make space.

You cannot heal in the same environment that made you sick. This may mean pulling back from certain responsibilities, stepping away from emotionally draining people, or saying no to new tasks until your soul regains strength. Healing requires time. It cannot be rushed.

2. Find support.

Every leader needs a safe place. Whether it is a counselor, a mentor, a peer, or a spiritual director, there must be someone with whom you can be completely honest. Vulnerability is not a threat to your ministry; it is a path to sustaining it. Many denominations and clergy associations offer confidential support services. Use them.

3. Surrender to the process.

Healing is not linear. It may involve counseling. It may require spiritual retreat. It may mean confronting old grief or trauma that has gone unresolved for years. It may be uncomfortable, but it is holy work. *"He restores my soul"* (Psalm 23:3) is not poetic, it is personal. Let Him do it.

You are not disqualified because you need help. You are not a failure because you're tired. You are simply a human, anointed and fragile, in need of the same grace you've poured into others.

There is a great deception in ministry that says healing must be private, hidden, and immediate. But biblical healing is often communal, gradual, and disruptive. Jesus healed publicly. He restored dignity as much as He restored function. And He never demanded people hide their suffering before they could be restored.

Why should it be different for leaders? To every wounded minister, this is the invitation: Come out of hiding. Your honesty is not a liability. It is your liberation. The healer who ignores their own pain eventually becomes numb. But the healer who seeks healing becomes whole, and whole leaders change the world.

Let the Lord tend to your wounds. Let the Spirit minister to your soul. Let the Church grow up enough to care for its shepherds. You have healed many. Now let God heal you.

11

Building a Healthier Church Culture

Churches are living ecosystems. They are not built on buildings or budgets, but on people, each with their own expectations, personalities, spiritual needs, and emotional patterns. And like any environment, the health of one part affects the whole. For ministry to be sustainable, we must recognize that clergy health and congregational culture are inseparably linked.

Far too often, ministry becomes a one-sided flow. The leader pours, the people receive. The pastor shows up, and the church watches. The shepherd feeds, but no one checks whether the shepherd is being fed. While this may appear functional on the surface, over time it creates a culture where leaders are celebrated for what they do but neglected for who they are.

Many pastors suffer silently not just because the work is hard, but because the culture around them does not make space for their humanity. Expectations are unspoken yet deeply felt. They are to be spiritual but not emotional, strong but never strained, present but never needing presence.

But what if churches could be taught to think differently? What if congregations were trained to honor not only the anointing but also the person who carries it? What if the body of Christ matured to the point where it protected its leaders, not just praised them?

This is the vision of a healthier church culture, a community where mutual care, emotional maturity, and shared responsibility are normal, not rare.

The Congregation's Role in Clergy Wellness

While pastors must steward their own well-being, the church has a biblical responsibility to care for its leaders. Paul wrote, *"Let the elders who rule well be considered worthy of double honor, especially those who labor in preaching and teaching"*(1 Timothy 5:17, ESV). Honor in this context is not merely about words or offerings. It includes respect, protection, and support.

A healthy church culture is one where honor is not just expressed on anniversaries or in appreciation services, it is lived out consistently. It looks like:

- Respecting the leader's time and personal boundaries
- Encouraging sabbaticals, rest days, and vacations without guilt
- Refraining from gossip or unrealistic comparisons
- Offering emotional support rather than endless demands
- Recognizing that pastors also grieve, struggle, and need care

In unhealthy church environments, leaders are often evaluated based on what they provide. If the preaching is strong, attendance is steady, and programs are running, people assume all is well. But churches must move beyond performance metrics and start asking deeper questions: *Is our pastor thriving emotionally? Does our leadership team feel supported? Have we created space for our leaders to breathe?*

In many cases, congregants unknowingly contribute to compassion fatigue. They assume availability means invincibility. They interpret a quick prayer as disinterest, not realizing their leader just came from a funeral or a counseling session with a suicidal member. They expect prompt responses to messages but never consider the hundreds of people vying for that same time.

A healthier church culture shifts this mindset. It teaches people that pastors are not superhuman. They are called, but still clay. They are gifted but still growing. And they too are part of the body, not separate from it.

Changing the Conversation: What Churches Must Teach

Many churches have never been taught how to care for their leaders. They've been taught how to receive ministry, but not how to reciprocate it. To build a culture of care, churches must begin talking openly about clergy wellness, not just behind closed doors, but in sermons, small groups, and leadership training.

Here are key truths that must be normalized:

1. **Ministry is emotionally taxing** – Just because a leader preaches with power does not mean they are not internally weary. Compassion fatigue is real, and it affects even the most faithful.

2. **Pastors need rest without guilt** – Taking time off is not selfish. It is biblical. *"Even youths grow tired and weary... but those who wait on the Lord will renew their strength"* (Isaiah 40:30–31, NIV).

3. **Support is more than applause** – Encouragement is not just "great sermon, pastor." It is offering help, asking about their well-being, respecting their family time, and being emotionally present.

4. **Conflict should be handled biblically** – Rather than venting frustrations among members, a healthy church addresses issues with grace and clarity. *"If your brother sins against you, go and tell him his fault, between you and him alone"* (Matthew 18:15, ESV). That includes pastors too.

5. **Spiritual leaders are not replacements for the Holy Spirit** – Congregants should not become dependent on their pastor for every answer or every crisis. They must be equipped to seek God for themselves, so the leader is not spiritually overburdened.

When churches are taught these truths, the dynamic shifts. The church no longer consumes its leaders. It becomes a safe place for them, a place where they can serve from fullness, not emptiness.

Shared Responsibility and Team Ministry

Another key to a healthy church culture is shared responsibility. The early church understood this. In Acts 6, when the apostles were overwhelmed by practical needs, they appointed deacons to share the load. The result? *"The word of God spread. The number of disciples in Jerusalem increased rapidly"* (Acts 6:7, NIV). Delegation did not slow the ministry, it expanded it.

Too many pastors are trying to carry too much because no one around them has been trained, or trusted, to help. But this is unsustainable. A healthy church raises up leaders, empowers volunteers, and spreads out the work.

This is not just practical, it is theological. The church is the body of Christ. No one part is designed to function alone. *"If one member suffers, all suffer together; if one member is honored, all rejoice together"* (1 Corinthians 12:26, ESV).

Every church should ask: Are we honoring our leaders by lifting with them? Or are we unknowingly increasing the weight they carry?

Equipping others to lead does not diminish the pastor's authority, it strengthens it. It allows the shepherd to focus on what only they can do: vision, spiritual oversight, and prayerful leadership. And it creates a healthier, more durable community.

Creating Safe Spaces for Leaders

Perhaps most importantly, healthy churches create safe spaces for their leaders to be human. That means:

- Letting pastors grieve when they experience personal loss
- Encouraging therapy or counseling as needed
- Understanding that not every prayer request can be responded to instantly
- Avoiding spiritual pedestal-building that isolates the leader

When a pastor says, “I need to step back for a moment,” the church should not panic. They should surround them. Pray for them. Affirm them. That’s not a sign of weakness. It is a sign of maturity.

The church should be the safest place in the world to admit, “I’m struggling.” But for too many leaders, it is the last place they’d ever say it. That must change.

It starts with humility on both sides. Leaders must be willing to open up, not to everyone, but to someone. And congregations must be willing to carry, not just be carried.

We often say the church is a family. If that’s true, then its leaders should never feel like orphans. They should never feel like hired hands performing for a crowd. They should feel like sons and daughters among brothers and sisters.

The burden of leadership will always exist, but it does not have to be crushing. When churches mature, when honor goes deeper than words, when support becomes tangible, when care becomes mutual, ministry becomes sustainable again.

The goal is not just effective churches. The goal is healthy ones. And healthy churches are built when everyone, including the pastor, is allowed to thrive.

How Congregations Can Support Their Leaders

A healthy church is never built on the strength of one person; it is built on the strength of a community. While God calls and equips leaders to shepherd His people, He never intended for pastors to carry the burden of ministry alone. Just as shepherds care for the flock, the flock also has a biblical responsibility to honor, support, and protect their leaders. A spiritually mature congregation recognizes that caring for the pastor is not optional — it is essential for the wellbeing of the entire church.

Paul reminded the church in Thessalonica, *"Esteem them very highly in love for their work's sake"* (1 Thessalonians 5:13, NKJV). This honor is not merely verbal; it is expressed through action, understanding, and shared responsibility. When a congregation supports its leaders well, compassion fatigue decreases, emotional health improves, and the church becomes a place where both shepherd and sheep can thrive.

1. Support Through Shared Responsibility

One of the most significant ways a congregation can reduce compassion fatigue is by sharing the load. Ministry cannot rest solely on the pastor, nor should the pastor be expected to attend to every crisis, every conflict, and every need.

Healthy churches:

- Develop volunteer teams
- Train intercessors and leaders
- Empower ministry departments
- Delegate pastoral care responsibilities appropriately

When the body functions as a body, the pastor is no longer the only functioning limb. As Moses learned in Exodus 18, shared leadership is not a luxury; it is a necessity.

2. Respecting Boundaries and Personal Time

Congregations can unintentionally contribute to exhaustion when they expect constant access to their leader. Honoring boundaries is an act of love. It communicates, "I value you as a person, not just for what you provide."

Practical ways congregations can honor boundaries:

- Respect pastoral days off
- Limit late-night calls to true emergencies
- Refrain from placing unrealistic emotional or spiritual demands
- Avoid expecting immediate responses to every text or message

When congregants respect healthy boundaries, pastors receive the mental space needed to hear God, rest, and remain emotionally whole.

3. Protecting the Pastor from Gossip, Criticism, and Unrealistic Expectations

One of the silent contributors to compassion fatigue is the emotional weight of navigating criticism, division, or internal conflict. Congregations play a vital role in cultivating a culture that uplifts rather than drains their leaders.

A healthy church:

- Refuses to entertain gossip about leadership
- Addresses concerns through proper biblical channels
- Speaks well of their leaders publicly and privately
- Extends grace instead of demanding perfection

Words can either build or break a leader. A supportive congregation guards the atmosphere so the pastor can lead with clarity and peace.

4. Encouraging Rest, Renewal, and Sabbatical

Pastors often feel guilty for resting, taking time away, or stepping back to recharge. A spiritually mature congregation does not just permit rest — it encourages it.

Church members can:

- Support sabbaticals
- Celebrate vacations instead of resenting them
- Ensure the pastor is not overloaded before or after time away
- Advocate for pastoral mental health and emotional wellbeing

When the congregation honors Sabbath rhythms, it releases the pastor to return refreshed, renewed, and able to lead with spiritual authority instead of fatigue.

5. Showing Appreciation and Emotional Support

Appreciation is not flattery; it is biblical encouragement. Paul said, *"Let the elders who rule well be counted worthy of double honor"*(1 Timothy 5:17, NKJV). Honor breathes life into weary leaders.

Support can include:

- A sincere "thank you"
- Prayer for the pastor and family
- Cards, meals, or small gestures of love
- Assistance during difficult seasons
- Recognizing the humanity of the leader

Every act of kindness becomes a reminder: *You are not alone.*

6. Protecting the Pastor's Family

Ministry is never experienced in isolation — it touches the spouse, children, and extended family. A congregation can reduce compassion fatigue by creating an environment that honors and protects the pastoral family.

Congregations should:

- Avoid placing unrealistic expectations on the spouse or children
- Provide privacy and safe spaces
- Offer support during family crises or transitions

- Acknowledge that the pastoral family needs grace just like any other

When the family is covered, the pastor can lead without constant internal conflict.

7. Praying Consistently for Leadership

Prayer is not supplemental; it is foundational. No congregation can truly support its leaders if it is not praying for them. Pastors fight visible and invisible battles, and intercession is one of the greatest gifts a church can offer.

Prayers should cover:

- Their emotional and spiritual strength
- Their marriage and children
- Protection from discouragement
- Wisdom for decision-making
- Fresh anointing and clarity of vision

A praying church sustains its pastor, strengthens the ministry, and closes the door to burnout.

A thriving church is not the result of a strong pastor alone but of a strong partnership between shepherd and sheep. When congregations intentionally support their leaders, the entire ministry becomes healthier, more united, and more effective. Compassion fatigue is not inevitable; many cases can be prevented when the people honor their leader, share responsibility, and cultivate an atmosphere of love, respect, and spiritual maturity. A church that cares for its pastor becomes a church where healing flows freely — not just to the leaders, but through them to everyone they serve.

12

The Leaders Self-Check Compassion Fatigue Guide

This chapter is a mirror, not for your ministry performance, but for your inner condition.

Too many leaders operate in survival mode, unaware of how deeply fatigue, frustration, and quiet suffering have taken root. This self-assessment is designed to help you pause and reflect: *How am I really doing?*

It is time to take inventory, not of your schedule or sermons, but of your soul.

Instructions:

For each statement below, rate yourself from **1 to 5**:

1 – Strongly Disagree

2 – Disagree

3 – Unsure/Neutral

4 – Agree

5 – Strongly Agree

The higher your score, the greater your risk of compassion fatigue or ministry-related burnout.

Emotional and Spiritual Strain

I feel emotionally numb or detached when ministering to others.

O-1 **O**- 2 **O**-3 **O**-4. **O**-5

I feel increasingly cynical, irritable, or discouraged about ministry.

O-1 **O**- 2 **O**-3 **O**-4. **O**-5

I often feel like I'm pretending to be okay when I'm not.

O-1 **O**- 2 **O**-3 **O**-4. **O**-5

I rarely feel spiritually refreshed, even after prayer or worship.

O-1 **O**- 2 **O**-3 **O**-4. **O**-5

I struggle to connect with God outside of ministry duties.

O-1 **O**- 2 **O**-3 **O**-4. **O**-5

Physical and Mental Exhaustion

I regularly feel drained, even after sleep or time off.

O-1 O- 2 O-3 O-4. O-5

I experience physical symptoms of stress (headaches, tension, insomnia).

O-1 O- 2 O-3 O-4. O-5

I push through exhaustion rather than allowing myself to rest.

O-1 O- 2 O-3 O-4. O-5

I cannot remember the last time I truly felt recharged.

O-1 O- 2 O-3 O-4. O-5

I've thought, *"If I could just disappear for a while, maybe I'd finally recover."*

O-1 O- 2 O-3 O-4. O-5

Isolation and Disconnection

I don't feel I have anyone I can be fully honest with about my struggles.

O-1 O- 2 O-3 O-4. O-5

I feel alone, even when surrounded by people.

O-1 O- 2 O-3 O-4. O-5

I keep my emotional pain hidden for fear of being judged or misunderstood.

O -1 O - 2 O -3 O -4. O -5

I struggle to maintain healthy relationships outside my ministry role.

O -1 O - 2 O -3 O -4. O -5

I feel emotionally distant from my spouse, children, or loved ones.

O -1 O - 2 O -3 O -4. O -5

Decreased Ministry Fulfillment

I no longer feel joy in ministry as I once did.

O -1 O - 2 O -3 O -4. O -5

I dread or avoid certain ministry tasks I used to enjoy.

O -1 O - 2 O -3 O -4. O -5

I sometimes resent the people I am called to serve.

O -1 O - 2 O -3 O -4. O -5

I often question whether I am still called or effective.

O -1 O - 2 O -3 O -4. O -5

I fantasize about leaving ministry altogether.

O-1 **O**- 2 **O**-3 **O**-4. **O**-5

Boundary Breakdown and Overextension

I say yes to ministry demands even when I am overextended.

O-1 **O**- 2 **O**-3 **O**-4. **O**-5

I feel guilty resting or taking time off.

O-1 **O**- 2 **O**-3 **O**-4. **O**-5

I frequently work through vacations, family time, or rest days.

O-1 **O**- 2 **O**-3 **O**-4. **O**-5

I believe the ministry would collapse if I stepped away.

O-1 **O**- 2 **O**-3 **O**-4. **O**-5

I avoid delegating because I don't fully trust others to lead.

O-1 **O**- 2 **O**-3 **O**-4. **O**-5

Personal and Family Pressures

My home life feels as stressful, or more stressful, than my ministry life.

O-1 **O**- 2 **O**-3 **O**-4. **O**-5

I often feel unable to rest because of ongoing family or personal problems.

O-1 O- 2 O-3 O-4. O-5

My spouse or children have expressed feeling neglected due to ministry demands.

O-1 O- 2 O-3 O-4. O-5

Financial struggles at home add significant stress to my ministry responsibilities.

O-1 O- 2 O-3 O-4. O-5

I often feel I must hide my family or personal struggles to protect my image as a leader.

O-1 O- 2 O-3 O-4. O-5

Scoring and Reflection

Total your score. Maximum possible: 150

- O **121–150 | Critical Zone**

  You are likely experiencing high compassion fatigue or approaching burnout. Immediate steps toward healing are necessary. You may need rest, counseling, medical attention, and deep spiritual renewal. This is not weakness; it is a call to restoration. You cannot pour from an empty vessel.

- ○ **91–120 | Warning Zone**

  You are functioning, but at a cost. Compassion fatigue is building. If left unaddressed, it could deepen into emotional or spiritual crisis. Begin making changes now, seek help, create space for recovery, and speak with trusted allies in leadership.

- ○ **61–90 | At-Risk Zone**

  You're holding on, but there are signs of overload. Your rhythms, boundaries, or emotional support systems may need to be reevaluated. Take this as an invitation to realign before deeper issues set in.

- ○ **31–60 | Balanced Zone**

  You appear to be in a sustainable rhythm, though occasional strain is present. Maintain your current practices and be intentional about rest, support, and soul care.

- ○ **0–30 | Healthy Zone**

  Your responses reflect strong emotional, spiritual, and physical health in ministry. Continue protecting this balance. Guard your boundaries and help foster health in those around you.

www.ingramcontent.com/pod-product-compliance
Lightning Source LLC
LaVergne TN
LVHW020648100826
845148LV00012B/2385
* 9 7 9 8 9 8 8 3 2 8 7 5 9 *